God Knows You're Talented

(even if YOU Don't)

Kara Eckmann Powell

Gospel Light
Gateway Christian Church

Gospel Light is an evangelical Christian publisher dedicated to serving the local church. We believe God's vision for Gospel Light is to provide church leaders with biblical, user-friendly materials that will help them evangelize, disciple and minister to children, youth and families.

We hope this Gospel Light resource will help you discover biblical truth for your own life and help you minister to youth. God bless you in your work.

For a free catalog of resources from Gospel Light please contact your Christian supplier or call 1-800-4-GOSPEL or at www.gospellight.com.

PUBLISHING STAFF
William T. Greig, Publisher
Dr. Elmer L. Towns, Senior Consulting Publisher
Dr. Gary S. Greig, Senior Consulting Editor
Jill Honodel, Editor
Pam Weston, Assistant Editor
Patti Virtue, Editorial Assistant
Kyle Duncan, Associate Publisher
Bayard Taylor, M.Div., Senior Editor, Theological and Biblical Issues
Barbara LeVan Fisher, Cover Designer
Debi Thayer, Designer

ISBN 0-8307-2355-2
© 1999 by Gospel Light
All rights reserved.
Printed in U.S.A.

HOW TO MAKE CLEAN COPIES FROM THIS BOOK

▼▼▼▼▼▼▼▼▼▼▼▼▼

YOU MAY MAKE COPIES OF PORTIONS OF THIS BOOK WITH A CLEAN CONSCIENCE IF:

- you (or someone in your organization) are the original purchaser;
- you are using the copies you make for a noncommercial purpose (such as teaching or promoting your ministry) within your church or organization;
- you follow the instructions provided in this book.

▼▼▼▼▼▼▼▼▼▼▼▼▼

HOWEVER, IT IS ILLEGAL FOR YOU TO MAKE COPIES IF:

- you are using the material to promote, advertise or sell a product or service other than for ministry fund-raising;
- you are using the material in or on a product for sale;
- you or your organization are **not** the original purchaser of this book.

By following these guidelines you help us keep our products affordable.
Thank you,
Gospel Light

CONTENTS

▼▼▼▼▼▼▼▼▼▼▼▼▼▼▼

HOW TO USE *GOD KNOWS YOU'RE TALENTED (EVEN IF YOU DON'T)*

▼▼▼▼▼▼▼▼▼▼▼▼▼

This 5- to 10-session course is designed to help junior-high students discover how to serve their King.

During this course students will discover or review that...

- God has given each believer special gifts, talents and abilities;
- Everyone is uniquely created to serve God;
- We should use our gifts and abilities to praise God and serve others;
- The whole Body of Christ is to use all of its gifts to serve together;
- God's greatest gift of all is salvation and we are to use our gifts to share His gospel with others.

You can use *God Knows You're Talented (Even if YOU Don't)* for Vacation Bible School, camp or retreat—or your regular youth fellowship meetings any time of the year. *God Knows You're Talented (Even if YOU Don't)* is designed to be a flexible course with the ability to expand from 5 to 10 sessions.

ABOUT INVOLVEMENT LEARNING

So often we hear or read accounts of youth who live empty lives and have no apparent goals or direction in life. To fill the emptiness, they often turn to activities that ultimately only heighten that emptiness. Now more than ever, today's youth need to know that the potential to live this dynamic kind of life is firmly rooted in the study of and obedience to God's Word.

It takes courage to live an obedient life and it takes strength to overcome the many barriers to Christian growth erected by the world. Therefore, it is not enough to simply tell today's youth that studying and obeying God's Word will lead to a productive life. Many teachers have helped their youth know this truth for themselves through involvement learning.

The teaching methods and materials in this book emphasize involvement learning. These methods will involve your students in the learning process and take them from the role of passively listening to one of actively digging into the Scriptures. These methods will help you create in your students the desire to examine God's Word and to make practical applications of the truths being studied.

Each session in this study includes three activities for each session:

- **Approach the Word**—involves students in activities that capture and direct their interest toward the theme of the session.

- **Bible Exploration**—students use a variety of methods to learn what the Bible says about the session's theme.
- **Conclusion and Decision**—involves each student in a discussion or activity that provides a way to apply the Bible truths to his or her own life.

Within each session is an option to expand the session to two meetings, making a total of 10 sessions. If you are using the five-session track, the following note gives you the directions at the end of the Bible Exploration:

Note: If you are completing this session in one meeting, ignore this break and skip to "Conclusion and Decision."

Immediately following this note you will find directions for expanding to a 10-session study:

Two-Meeting Track: If you want to spread this session over two meetings, STOP here and close in prayer. Inform students of the content to be covered in your next meeting.

The **Two-Meeting Track** box is then followed by:
- **Review and Approach**—gives an opportunity for review of the previous lesson and an introduction to the Bible Exploration Two;
- **Bible Exploration Two**—further expands on the Bible study of the previous session.

The ideas provided in these sessions may stimulate additional ideas of your own that fit your group and teaching style. It is our prayer that the learning experiences suggested in this book, coupled with the power of God's Word, will challenge and motivate your students—encouraging some to become Christians and stirring up those who have grown complacent in their spiritual lives.

INTRODUCING YOUNG PEOPLE TO CHRIST
▼▾▼▾▼▾▼▾▼▾▼▾▼

How do you present Christ to a young person?

1. **Pray.** Ask God to prepare the hearts of students to receive the message and prepare you to present it.

2. **Lay the foundation.** Youth are evaluating you and the Lord you serve by everything you do and say. They are looking for people in whose lives knowing God makes a noticeable difference, for people who love them and listen to them—the same way God loves them and listens to them.

   Learn to listen with your full attention. Learn to share honestly both the joys and the struggles you encounter as a Christian. Be honest about your own questions and about your personal concern for students. Learn to accept teens as they are. Christ died for them while they were yet sinners. You are also called to love them as they are.

3. **Be aware of opportunities.** A student may ask to talk after class. Or some might be waiting for you to suggest going for a soda—getting alone together where you can share what Jesus Christ means to you.

4. **Have a plan.** Don't lecture or force the issue. Here are some tips to keep in mind:

   - **Put the student at ease.** Be perceptive of feelings and remember he or she is probably nervous. Be relaxed, natural and casual in your conversation, not critical or judgmental.

   - **Get the student to talk**, and listen carefully to what is said. Students sometimes make superficial or shocking statements just to get your reaction. Don't begin lecturing or problem solving. Instead encourage him or her to keep talking.

   - **Be gently direct.** Students may have trouble bringing up the topic. If you sense this, a simple question like, "How are you and God getting along?" can unlock a life-changing conversation.

   - **Discuss God's desire to have fellowship with people.** As you relate the plan God has for enabling people to have a relationship with Him, move through the points slowly enough to allow time for thinking and comprehending. However, do not drag out the presentation:
     a. God's goal for us is abundant life (see John 3:16; 10:10).
     b. All people are separated from God by sin (see Romans 3:23; 6:23).

c. God's solution is Jesus Christ who died to pay the penalty for our sin (see John 14:6; Romans 5:8).

d. Our response is to receive Christ as Savior (see John 1:12).

- **Make sure the student understands that accepting Christ is very simple,** though very profound. If you feel the student understands, ask if he or she would like to accept Christ now. If so, ask the student to pray with you. Explain that praying is simply talking to God. In this case it's telling God of the student's need for Christ and desire for Christ to be in his or her life as personal Lord and Savior. Then suggest that the student study in order to begin growing in the faith.

   If the student feels unready to make a decision, suggest some Scripture to read and make an appointment to get together again. John 14—16; Romans 3—8 and the Gospel of Mark are good sections of Scripture for reading. Pray for the student in the meantime.

5. **Remember your responsibility is simply to present the gospel** and to be able to explain the hope that is within you. It is the Holy Spirit who makes the heart ready for a relationship with God and gives growth.

WHEN IT'S ALL SAID AND DONE

When it's all said and done, what is done will far outlast what is said.

The time you invest in building relationships, encouraging and affirming students, listening to them and putting up with their rowdy moods (which seem to be never ending) will pay dividends in the kingdom of God.

It is the personal touch that does it. Kids know when someone cares for them. It shows. It pays off. It declares loudly, "Here is a real person who has a real relationship with Christ, who wants to know the real you."

Relationships should not end with the packing away of materials. New contacts have been made during these days. These contacts need to be followed up.

Plan follow-up for those who become Christians. Get them into Sunday School. Visit their homes to answer questions and give encouragement. Provide transportation when needed.

Plan follow-up for those who rededicate their lives to the Lord. They need guidance in Bible study, in prayer and in preparing for the work the Lord has for them.

Plan follow-up for the unsaved. Invite them to church youth activities. Bring them to Sunday School and worship services. Continue to pray for them by name and keep in touch with them. Remember birthdays with a card or phone call.

Plan follow-up for unchurched parents. Show genuine interest in their young people. Continue to invite the entire family to church services and church activities—especially to adult Bible classes.

And when that once ornery student begins to respond to the love and caring you have shown, don't be surprised if he or she thinks about you and what you did to demonstrate God's love—and then tries to do the same for someone else.

▼
▼
▼
▼
▼
▼
▼
▼
▼
▼
▼
▼
▼
▼
▼
▼

THE NERVE TO SERVE

LEADER'S DEVOTIONAL

▼▼▼▼▼▼▼▼▼▼▼

"I'm just a junior higher. I can't even drive, let alone do anything important. There's no way I can change stuff and if I tried, my friends would think I was dorky."

Just a junior higher, huh? Hardly. Even though some, if not most, or maybe all of your students can relate to the insecurity and hopelessness of being "just" a junior higher, this course is going to try to erase the "just." The goal of every session in this book is to unleash the incredible potential junior highers have to be changed by Christ to change the world.

Hopefully you really believe that and don't view junior-high ministry simply as glorified baby-sitting. You may never know what the students who sit in front of you are capable of. After all, the great evangelist Billy Graham was thirteen years old once. So was Mother Teresa. So was your senior pastor. And so were you.

This course gives you the chance to speak words of life and hope to students who sit awkwardly in front of you each week, too timid to believe they have anything to add to the world around them. Make a commitment with your entire adult leadership team to fill this series with an attitude of contagious confidence. After all, there is no such thing as *just* a junior higher and there is no such thing as *just* a junior-high teacher.

SESSION 1

KEY VERSES

"His master replied, 'Well done, good and faithful servant! You have been faithful with a few things; I will put you in charge of many things. Come and share your master's happiness.'" Matthew 25:21

BIBLICAL BASIS

Matthew 25:14-30; 1 Peter 4:10

FOCUS OF THIS SESSION

God wants us to use the gifts, talents and abilities that He has given us.

AIMS OF THIS SESSION

During this session students will:

- Examine Christ's challenge to put to use every talent that God has given them;
- Discover a creative application for any and every talent they have;
- Identify one talent they can use this week.

APPROACH THE WORD

(15 MINUTES)

OBJECTIVE

To help students understand how wrong it is to refuse to use a gift that has been given to them.

MATERIALS AND PREPARATION NEEDED

- ❑ Streamers
- ❑ Balloons

❑ Festive music and a player

❑ A birthday card

❑ A boxed gift that is wrapped in colorful wrapping paper and ribbons

Ahead of time, call one student or adult staff member and explain that you would like to honor him or her with a "Surprise Birthday Party." Since many junior highers feel awkward in the midst of public attention, make sure you choose a student who enjoys being the center of the group's attention. Ideally, it would also be someone who has a birthday relatively near the date of this lesson. Explain that you want the honoree to come to your class 10 minutes late so that the rest of the students can "surprise" him or her. Ask him/her to act truly shocked and surprised. Then you will give him/her a wrapped gift that he/she is to unwrap and then complain about how he/she will "never use this" because he/she already has one, doesn't like the color, etc. You may want to agree together on the gift that the honoree will be opening, such as a book, compact disc or cookies, so he/she can think of several reasons ahead of time to explain to the class why he/she won't use the gift.

Before students arrive, decorate the room with streamers and balloons. Set up the music player.

SURPRISE!

As your students arrive, have the room well lit and upbeat music playing to create a welcoming atmosphere. Ask students to contribute toward the gift (if they are able to) and to sign the birthday card. Begin your lesson by explaining: **Today we're going to have a surprise birthday party for** _____ (insert prearranged person's name here). **We're going to hide in various places around the room and when he/she walks in, jump out, yell "Surprise" and start singing "Happy Birthday" to him/her.**

Once your student arrives and your class has yelled "Surprise" and sung "Happy Birthday," gather the class together so that you can give the wrapped gift to the honoree. Once he/she opens the gift, ask, **"How do you like it?"** At this point, he/she should start making a list of reasons he/she can't use the gift. You should act somewhat hurt and try to explain a few reasons why he/she can use the gift (i.e., "It's not that bad," or "Maybe you'll eventually like the color"). But he/she should continue to act disappointed and refuse to take the gift.

SESSION 1

By this time, the rest of your students will probably feel somewhat awkward and uncomfortable as they watch this stubborn ingratitude. At this point, explain that this whole "Surprise Birthday Party" was an act and that the honoree knew in advance that he/she was supposed to complain and refuse to take the gift.

Ask: **Have you ever given someone a gift and felt like he or she probably didn't like it very much? How did you feel?** Allow a minute or two to discuss their feelings.

God gives us gifts all of the time, but often we're just like our friend here. We whine and refuse to accept and use them. How do you think that makes God feel?

Today we're going to begin a series to learn how to identify and put to use every single gift God has given us.

BIBLE EXPLORATION

(45 MINUTES)

OBJECTIVE

To help students grasp the importance of using the gifts God has given them to serve others.

MATERIALS AND PREPARATION NEEDED

- ☐ Make five photocopies of "The Toolbox" on pages 23-25
- ☐ White board, chalkboard, overhead projector and transparency or newsprint and pens or chalk
- ☐ A copy of *The Message* by Eugene Peterson (NavPress, 1993)
- ☐ Collect the props listed on the script

Several days before the class session, ask four students (or adults) to prepare the skit ahead of time.

THE TOOLBOX

Begin the lesson by asking, **What are some of the gifts or talents you**

admire in other people? Write the students' responses on a white board, chalkboard, overhead or newsprint. Most will share the obvious ones: good looks, intelligence, musical, artistic or athletic ability. Encourage them to come up with the less obvious gifts as well, such as leadership, speaking, mechanical, or mathematical abilities; ability to make friends, to make people laugh or to encourage people, etc. Keep the list to use later.

Ask: **What would happen if a great athlete quit practicing and training for a few years, then ran out on the field and tried to play?** Allow a few responses, then ask: **What would happen if a great musician stopped performing and practicing for a few years, then walked out on stage to give a concert?** After a few responses, say: **God has given each of us unique gifts. What do you think would happen if we didn't use our gifts? Let's find out.**

Have the "actors" perform the skit, then discuss the following:
What was Barry given and who gave it to him?
Why did he refuse to help the three people?
Was he wrong or right in his refusal? (Have students explain their answers.)
Have you been in a situation where you had something or some ability you were afraid to use? What happened?

Remember our first activity? God has given us gifts for a special purpose. **What is that special purpose?** Ask for their responses, then ask: **What do you think would happen if we didn't use the gifts God has given us? Let's find out what God's Word says.** Have someone with a good reading voice read Matthew 25:14-30 from *The Message* version of the Bible by Eugene Peterson. (If you cannot obtain a copy, use *The Living Bible* version.) Then discuss:
Who is the master? Who are the servants?
Why were the first two servants rewarded?
What happened to the third servant? How is he like Barry in the skit?
How does this parable relate to the gifts we are given by God?
What does it teach us about the unique abilities that God gives each of us?
Why does God give us special gifts? (To serve others and ultimately to lead others to Him.)

Divide students into groups of three or four. Assign each small group three of the special gifts or abilities that you and the students listed at the beginning of the lesson. Say: **Pretend you know someone who has these three special gifts or abilities. How could that person serve God using all three gifts? You will have two minutes to come up**

with as many ways in which that person could put those gifts to use for God's kingdom. Encourage them to be creative. When time is up, ask each group to share at least one way that someone with their assigned abilities could serve others.

Note: If you are completing this session in one meeting, ignore this break and skip to "Conclusion and Decision."

Two-Meeting Track: If you want to spread this session over two meetings, STOP here and close in prayer. Inform students of the content to be covered in your next meeting.

REVIEW AND APPROACH

(15 MINUTES)

OBJECTIVE

To help students discover that serving others might not be easy.

MATERIALS AND PREPARATION NEEDED

- ❑ Masking tape
- ❑ Chocolate ice cream
- ❑ Vanilla ice cream
- ❑ Strawberry ice cream
- ❑ Marshmallow cream
- ❑ Chocolate sauce
- ❑ Peanuts
- ❑ Rainbow sprinkles
- ❑ Maraschino cherries
- ❑ A plastic tarp
- ❑ Cardboard

❑ A tennis racket that can get very messy

❑ Two extra large T-shirts that can also get very messy

❑ Something to cover yourself if you don't want to get messy

Ahead of time, cover the head and strings of the tennis racket with cardboard so that it is impermeable. Lay out the plastic tarp to protect the room. If possible, this activity might best be done outside where everything could be hosed off when finished!

ICE CREAM ANYONE?

Ask: **Who likes to play tennis? Who likes ice cream sundaes? I need two volunteers who like to play tennis, like ice cream, and don't mind getting a little messy.** Ideally, you would have one girl and one guy volunteer. Give both volunteers the T-shirts to put on and spread the tarp out on the ground. Put a piece of masking tape approximately four feet from you as you explain: **Today we're going to talk about serving, and we're going to start by doing a little tennis serving. One at a time, these friends are going to toss these ice cream sundae items to me, and I will serve them back to them by hitting the items with my tennis racket in their direction. Instead of dodging away from the flying ice cream sundae ingredients, they want to get as messy as possible, so they will want to move toward the ice cream and toppings that come flying their way. The goal is to make two human ice cream sundaes.** One item at a time, have each volunteer toss a handful or two of each of the following in your direction so you can hit it back to them: chocolate ice cream, vanilla ice cream, strawberry ice cream, marshmallow cream, chocolate sauce, whole peanuts, rainbow sprinkles, and maraschino charries. It's going to be messy, but junior highers love messes, especially food messes, so don't be afraid of a little bit of food chaos. Have a prize (possibly a carton of ice cream or at least an ice cream bar) for the student who gets the messiest.

Explain: **We learned last time that God has given each of us special gifts for a purpose. What is that purpose?** (To serve others and bring them to the Lord.) After someone has answered, explain further: **Serving is not always easy. In fact, our two friends here might say serving is sometimes "messy." But serving God is rewarding when we see His results.**

Today we're going to continue to talk about gifts. But our eventual goal is to do more than just talk about gifts. By the end of today,

you'll be able to figure out how to take one specific gift that God has given you and use it to serve others.

BIBLE EXPLORATION TWO

(45 MINUTES)

OBJECTIVE

To help students brainstorm all of the ways they can use the varied talents God has already given them and will eventually give them.

MATERIALS AND PREPARATION NEEDED

- ❑ Pens or pencils
- ❑ Index cards
- ❑ A bag
- ❑ White board, chalkboard or overhead projector and pens or chalk
- ❑ **Option:** Video camera and blank video tape, with VCR and TV to show the video

WHATEVER GIFTS

Ask for a volunteer to read 1 Peter 4:10 aloud. After the volunteer is finished, write the first part of the verse on a white board, chalkboard or overhead from the *New International Version* of the Bible: "Each one should use whatever gift he has received to serve others." Circle the word "whatever" and explain: **Notice that Scripture says "whatever gift." I want you to get into groups of five or six.** After they have done so, distribute pens and 10 index cards to each group and explain: **I want you to make a list of all of the wild talents and gifts that God gives people. Be as creative as you can—from juggling to hairstyling to skateboarding. Select one person in your group to write your suggestions on the index cards. Write each gift on a separate index card.**

After five minutes, collect all of the index cards and place them all in the same bag. Ask the group member who has the longest hair in each group to come and pick seven index cards out of the bag without looking at the cards. It doesn't matter whether or not the index cards they pick originated from their group. After each group's representative has drawn seven cards, divide any leftover cards among the groups.

Explain: **I'm going to give you 10 minutes to create your own drama sketch as a group using the gifts and talents written on the cards you have picked. Your goal is to make some sort of a story about a person, or people, who have the selected talents and is using them to serve others. There are only three rules. First, every card must be used. Second, every person in the group must be involved in the sketch. Third, have fun.**

After ten minutes, have each group perform their drama. Make sure each group receives a lot of applause both before and after they perform their drama. Since junior highers love seeing themselves on video, try videotaping each group so you can show the dramas at a later date.

CONCLUSION AND DECISION

▼▽▼▽▼▽▼▽▼▽▼▽▼▽▼▽▼

(10 MINUTES)

OBJECTIVE

To give students the time to think of one talent they can use this week to serve others.

MATERIALS AND PREPARATION NEEDED

- ❑ Approximately five pennies per student
- ❑ A cup or similar container to hold the pennies
- ❑ A felt-tip pen
- ❑ A container that can be written on, such as a cardboard paint bucket or a large styrofoam cup
- ❑ Tape or CD of worship music and a player

USING YOUR TALENTS

Take a few pennies in your hand and hold the penny container in the other hand, then explain: **Sometimes junior highers think that they** don't have many talents at all. That's a lie. As we saw in the parable of the talents, each of you has talents that can be used to serve others. Each penny represents a talent that God has given you. The container is your commitment to use your talents to serve others this week. We're going to pass around the pennies first. Take as many pennies as you want, one for each specific talent you want to commit to using to serve others this week. For example, if you have the talents of being good with children and encouraging a depressed friend, take two pennies. Then we're going to pass around this second container and a pen. Take the pen and write the talents you are committing to use on the outside of the container, then put the corresponding number of pennies inside the container. As the teacher, you start first by taking a few pennies to correspond to a few talents in your own life. Write the specific talents on the container and then place the pennies inside the container. You may want to play worship music during this exercise.

After the pennies and container have circulated around the room, close in a time of prayer, thanking God for every single talent He has given these junior highers. Hold up the container with all of the diverse talents written on it and explain: **What a cool variety of gifts God has given us. Next time we're going to learn more about our unique gifts.**

THE TOOLBOX

▼ ▼ ▼ ▼ ▼ ▼ ▼ ▼ ▼ ▼ ▼ ▼ ▼

USING GOD'S GIFTS TO SERVE HIM

Characters

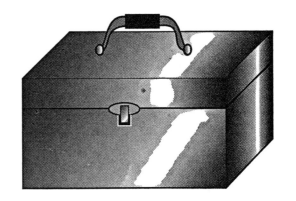

Barry, a teenager
Homeless Lady
Grease Monkey, a mechanic
Skateboarder

Props

A large shiny toolbox with a few tools inside to make noise
Old, frumpy clothes for Homeless Lady
A can of tuna
A coin
Oily overalls and cap for Grease Monkey
A skateboard
A trash can partially filled with newspapers

Barry runs onstage, carrying a large, shiny toolbox.

Barry: (*Calling offstage*) Dad! Wai...DAD! Hold up, will ya! You spaced your tool...I said you forgot your toolbox!

(*He tries to catch his breath.*) No, YOU forgot it!

(*He stops and looks puzzled.*) What d'you mean? Wait. Time out. What do I want with this thing?

(*Pauses, looking as though he is listening to someone.*) No, no, Dad, it's your toolbox. Awww, is this one of those "You're a man now, you need your OWN toolbox" routines? Okay, so it's mine now. Fine. So how long you gonna be gone? Dad? DAD!

(*Looking dejected, he looks at the toolbox.*) Man, this is just great! Why couldn't he pull the old "You're a man now, you need your own Forerunner"?

(*He looks around, then carefully opens the toolbox.*) What am I doing? No way. I touch it and something's gonna break. Guaranteed. (*He looks down and carefully closes the toolbox.*) Yeah, if something happens to anything before he gets back, I'll just tell him I didn't touch a pickin' thing. That's my story.

Homeless Lady enters from the opposite side of the stage. **Barry** picks up the toolbox and walks toward her. As he passes by the **Homeless Lady,** he tries to ignore her.

Homeless Lady: Hey. Hey, bub. Hey, pally.

Barry: Got no change. (*Keeps walking.*)

Homeless Lady: Nice toolbox. Wait, wait. (*She digs in her pocket and pulls out a can of tuna.*) Ya gotta can opener on ya?

Barry: (*Stops and rolls eyes sarcastically as he looks at her.*) Sure. In my back pocket.

Homeless Lady: Where'd you get the toolbox?

Barry: From my father. What do you care?

Homeless Lady: Whadda ya got in it?

Barry: I don't know.

Homeless Lady: Ain't ya looked in it even?

Barry: What's it to you, lady!? (*Digs in pocket.*) Look, I think I do have a quarter.

Homeless Lady: Maybe there's a can opener in there. Ya never know. Why'n'cha open'er up and see?

Barry: Trust me. There's no can opener in here!

Homeless Lady: Maybe I could use a screwdriver and a hammer or somethin', huh?

Barry: Here, here's a quarter. I'm not opening the toolbox, okay!

Homeless Lady: (*Walks away, mumbling.*) Why you carry the thing around if ya ain't gonna use it? Sheesh!

Grease Monkey: (*Offstage, yells*): Hey pal! Hey buddy! Wait a minute!

Barry turns around as **Grease Monkey** enters from the opposite side of the stage wearing oily overalls and cap.

Grease Monkey: Hey, you got a trimensional dual-sided spanner in that kit there?

Barry: Sorry, guy. You can't save the world today.

Grease Monkey: Hey, no really, ya mind I take a look? It'd really help me out. (*He heads toward Barry who backs away, hugging his toolbox.*)

Barry: Get away. You're not looking in my toolbox.

Grease Monkey: Come on. That's a spiffy lookin' kit there. I'm broke down back there! One look. Please!

Barry: Look! I'm not opening the toolbox! My dad gave it to me. It's his, got it? I'm not gonna use nothing!

Grease Monkey: If your dad gave it to ya, then I'm sure he wouldn't mind…

Barry: He minds!

Grease Monkey: (*Throws his hands up in surrender.*) Okay, okay! Don't get all squirrelly!

Grease Monkey walks offstage. **Skateboarder** enters from the opposite side of the stage carrying a skateboard and looking at the wheels as though something is wrong. He looks up, sees Barry and comes up behind him. **Barry** doesn't notice him at first. He turns around and yells in surprise and almost drops the toolbox.

Skateboarder: Nice toolbox, dude. You think you got a…

Barry: NO!

Skateboarder: Maybe a wrench or some…

Barry: Nothing!

Skateboarder: Then what's that there? (*Points to toolbox.*)

Barry: (*Backing away, protects the toolbox.*) A mistake, that's what it is! Somebody just gave it to me. I didn't know I was gonna have to do something with it!

Skateboarder: Well, hey, can I have it then?

Barry: No! It's mine! Leave me alone.

Skateboarder: Unbelievable. (*Looks at the box.*) I don't need this grief. None of it!

Barry: (*He looks around and sees the trash can. He walks over and stuffs the toolbox in and covers it up with newspapers.*) That'll work. When he comes back, I'll go get the stupid toolbox for him. He oughta be grateful, anyways. It'll all be in great shape when he gets it back. (*Pause. Wipes his hands.*) Yeah, he should be real happy I took nooo chances with it.

Barry taps the trash can twice and walks offstage, hands stuffed in his pockets.[1]

Blackout

Note:

1. Adapted from Lawrence G. and Andrea J. Enscoe, "The Right Equipment" taken from *Skit'omatic* (Ventura, Calif.: Gospel Light, 1993), pp. 74-75.

▼
▼
▼
▼
▼
▼
▼
▼
▼
▼
▼
▼
▼
▼
▼

ONE OF A KIND

LEADER'S DEVOTIONAL

▼▼▼▼▼▼▼▼▼▼▼▼▼

Kim wishes she had Ian's awesome singing voice.

Ian wishes he had Chad's ability to get past any soccer defense and score at least three goals per game.

Chad wishes he had Clara's brain in science class so that he could get the top score in every test.

Clara wishes everyone thought she was as responsible as Kim so that she could get as many baby-sitting jobs as Kim did.

Kim, Ian, Chad and Clara are all seventh graders in the same church. Like most junior highers (and many adults), they long for what is just beyond their reach and ignore what God has already handed them.

Your junior highers need to understand that the fact that there is no one like them is not a bad thing. It is a good thing. Just like the diversity of flowers enhances the garden's beauty and the variety of mountain peaks adds to a mountain range's majesty, so do the unique qualities of each of your junior highers increase the potential of your ministry. The goal of this session is to help students understand that each of them is unique. One of a kind. Special. Unparalleled. Never to be repeated. Pray that God would burn that truth into every one of your students' minds, hearts and souls this week.

SESSION 2

KEY VERSES

▼▼▼▼▼▼▼▼▼▼▼

"There are different kinds of gifts, but the same Spirit. There are different kinds of service, but the same Lord." 1 Corinthians 12:4,5

BIBLICAL BASIS

▼▼▼▼▼▼▼▼▼▼▼

1 Corinthians 12:1-11; Romans 12:4-8; Ephesians 4:11,12; Philippians 2:17

FOCUS OF THIS SESSION

▼▼▼▼▼▼▼▼▼▼▼

We are each uniquely created as useful vessels of God.

AIMS OF THIS SESSION

▼▼▼▼▼▼▼▼▼▼▼

During this session students will:

• Examine the variety of spiritual gifts the apostle Paul describes in 1 Corinthians 12:1-11;

• Discover one to three of their own spiritual gifts;

• Identify each other's gifts and encourage one another to use them.

APPROACH THE WORD

▼▼▼▼▼▼▼▼▼▼▼

(20 MINUTES)

OBJECTIVE

To help students realize that each of them is created one of a kind.

MATERIALS AND PREPARATION NEEDED

❑ Photocopies of "One of a Kind" on page 37, one copy for every four students

❑ Pens or pencils

ONE OF A KIND

Greet your junior highers warmly at the start of this lesson. Explain: **Today I'm going to let you know a few things about me that you probably don't know.** Give a few random facts about yourself such as where you were born, your favorite television show, your favorite ice cream flavor, or what you would do if you inherited one million dollars. After each fact, ask if there are any others who share that same characteristic.

Explain: **Today we're going to learn a whole lot more about each other. I'd like you to get into groups of four.** Distribute a pen or pencil and a copy of "One of a Kind" to each group and ask: **Do you see the four sections around the edges of the paper numbered one, two, three and four? Put one group member's name on the line in each numbered section. The goal of this game is to come up with as many one-of-a-kind things about each group member as you can. The way you do this is to start discussing things you like, things you dislike, your family background, what you want to do in your future, etc. If you are the only person who has that characteristic, write that characteristic in the section with your name. If all four of you share the same characteristic, write that in the center box. Make sure that each person has at least one thing written in his or her section and the group has at least two things written in the center box by the time we finish.**

Give students 7 to 10 minutes to complete this exercise. If you have less than 15 students, ask each person to share one of his or her one-of-a-kind characteristics with the whole group. If you have more than 15 students, ask for volunteers to share one of their one-of-a-kind characteristics.

Transition to the rest of the lesson by saying: **Look around the room. There is no one else like you. God has made you special and He has given you special characteristics and gifts. By the end of today, you are going to be excited about how special and unique you are.**

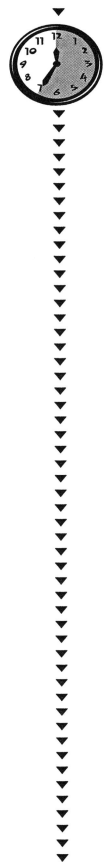

SESSION 2

BIBLE EXPLORATION

(35 MINUTES)

OBJECTIVE

To help students understand each gift Paul described in 1 Corinthians 12:1-11.

MATERIALS AND PREPARATION NEEDED

- ☐ Stopwatch
- ☐ A copy of "Gifts Galore" on page 38
- ☐ Three sheets of poster board
- ☐ Tape
- ☐ Pens

GIFTS GALORE

Divide your group into one girls' group and one guys' group and explain: **Today we're going to play "Gift Charades." Who has played Charades before? Who can explain it?** After the volunteer explains how to play Charades, clarify any points that need further explanation, then continue: **That's right, we'll ask for volunteers who will act out for their own gender some of the gifts God gives us. With this stopwatch I will time how long it takes before one of their group members guesses the gift. Remember the person acting out the gift can't say anything at all.**

One at a time, ask for volunteers to come and act out a gift. You will give them the gift to act out by whispering one in their ear from the "Gifts Galore" resource. Keep a running total of the time it takes each group to guess their assigned gifts.

At the end of the game, congratulate the winning gender and transition to 1 Corinthians 12:1-11 by explaining: **I didn't just make up those gifts. They came right out of Scripture.**

Ask for a volunteer to read Paul's explanation of gifts from 1 Corinthians 12:1-11. Tape the three poster board sheets to the wall and explain: **That's a pretty long list of gifts. Let's divide the gifts up into shorter lists. We'll use one of three words to describe each gift.**

The first is "Love." Lots of the gifts Paul writes about relate to how we love each other. The second is "Power." These power gifts are some of the cool and dramatic ways we see God's power in action. The third is "Word." These are gifts that involve an understanding of God's Word to us—the Bible.

Write either "Love," "Power" or "Word" on each poster board. Explain: **Let's go back through 1 Corinthians 12:7-10 as well as other gifts Paul mentions in Romans 12:4-8 and Ephesians 4:11,12 and see where these gifts fit in our lists of "Love," "Power" or "Word."** One at a time, read the verses and name the gifts. Then ask students which key word best fits that gift, and then write that gift on that list. Some gifts can easily fit in two lists, so feel free to write them in multiple lists. Your lists should resemble something like the following (note the overlap in the lists):

- Love: serving, encouraging, giving, mercy, healing
- Power: wisdom, knowledge, faith, healing, miracles, prophecy, distinguishing between spirits, tongues and the interpretation of tongues.
- Word: teaching, leadership, prophecy, apostle, evangelist, pastor

Note: If you are completing this session in one meeting, ignore this break and skip to "Conclusion and Decision."

Two-Meeting Track: If you want to spread this session over two meetings, STOP here and close in prayer. Inform students of the content to be covered in your next meeting.

SESSION 2

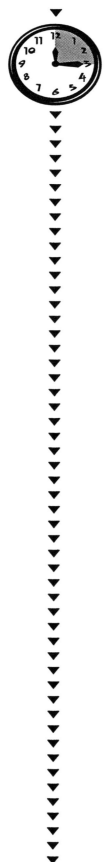

REVIEW AND APPROACH

(15 MINUTES)

OBJECTIVE

To help students begin to understand what Paul means by being poured out as a drink offering.

MATERIALS AND PREPARATION NEEDED

- ❑ Several large plastic trash bags, one for every eight students
- ❑ Several spoons
- ❑ One straw per student
- ❑ Small plastic or paper cups
- ❑ Eight various type of drinks, such as nonfat milk, apple juice, sugar water, fruit punch, cola, tea, coffee, lemonade
- ❑ **Suggestion:** Ask several parents to help with this activity. You will need one adult for each team of eight students.

Ahead of time, you need to pour a bit of each of your drinks into separate cups. To figure out the number of cups you need, take the number of students you expect and divide the number by eight (for example, if you expect 40 students, divide 40 by eight to come up with five cups of each type of drink).

SLURPY RELAY

Ask: **How many of you are thirsty?** As you lay down the plastic trash bags, ask students to form teams of eight (or four, if you have less than 15 students). Assign one adult or responsible student to pour drinks for each group (this may mean calling parents in advance and asking them to attend your session).

Have team members line up about 15 to 20 feet from the trash bags facing their team's bag. **Option:** The trash bags could be placed on tables.

Explain: **Today we are all going to get a little drink. We're going to play a slurping relay. The adult volunteer who is assigned to your team is going to pour out a little drink for each of you during the relay. Each of you is going to get a different drink, and you can't run back to tag the next person on your team until you have correctly whispered the name of your drink in the adult's ear. Once you do this, you may return to your team, tag the next person in line and that person will do the same thing. Repeat the process until everyone on your team has participated.**

There is a trick to this relay. Instead of letting you drink out of cups, your adult volunteer is going to put five spoonfuls of the drink from the cup onto an area of the plastic bag that has been assigned to your team. Then your adult will hand you a straw to use to suck up all of the drink from the plastic bag. Once you have finished slurping, you try to guess what it is. If you guess it incorrectly, your adult volunteer pours two more spoonfuls on the plastic bag and you keep guessing and slurping until you have figured out what it is.

Instruct the adults that they can give hints if needed. So each person runs to the plastic bag, gets a straw, slurps the drink, then guesses what the drink is. Once the person gives the correct answer, he or she runs back to his or her team and tags the next person.

After the game has finished, you may want to have several two-liter bottles or cans of soda to give the winning team.

Explain: **All of these beverages have one thing in common. They can quench thirst. Paul writes in Philippians 2:17 that he is happy to serve others by being poured out like a drink offering. The drink offering was poured out on the altar daily by the Jewish priests in the Temple as a sacrifice to God. So Paul was saying that he was glad to sacrifice himself to serve others for God. Paul understood the gifts God gives and he knew that each time he used his gifts, other people were helped. But just like each drink is a little different, each one of us is also a little different and we are poured out in different ways. Today we are going to study the different ways our gifts can be poured out to help others.**

SESSION 2

BIBLE EXPLORATION TWO

▼▼▼▼▼▼▼▼▼▼▼▼▼

(45 MINUTES)

OBJECTIVE

To enable students to identify one to three of their own spiritual gifts.

MATERIALS AND PREPARATION NEEDED

- ❑ Photocopies of "The Spiritual Gifts Discovery" on pages 39-40, one per student
- ❑ Photocopies of "My Own Gifts" on page 41, one per student
- ❑ Pens or pencils

MY OWN GIFTS

Explain: **Last time we looked at the gifts Paul described in Romans 12, 1 Corinthians 12, and Ephesians 4. What gifts can you remember from these passages?**

Explain: **Every single one of these gifts is still in operation today. How is that possible? Because they operate in each of you. Each of you has a unique combination of gifts that can be poured out. I'm going to give you a copy of "The Spiritual Gifts Discovery" and a pen. You are to evaluate each sentence and decide how well it describes you on a scale of zero to three. If the sentence really describes you, write a three next to it. If it somewhat describes you, write a two next to it. If it describes you just a bit, write a one next to it. If it doesn't describe you at all, write a zero next to it. I'll let you know what to do when you finish.**

Once students have finished, distribute a copy of "My Own Gifts" to each student. Explain: **In the spaces below, write the number of your response to that statement from "The Spiritual Gifts Discovery" next to the corresponding number. Then add up the two numbers you have recorded in each row and place the sum in the total column.**

Ask: **What were some of your gifts with the biggest numbers? Do you agree that these might be some of the unique gifts God has given you?**

CONCLUSION AND DECISION
▼▼▼▼▼▼▼▼▼▼▼▼▼▼
(15 MINUTES)

OBJECTIVE

To help students get in the practice of identifying and encouraging each other to use their gifts.

MATERIALS AND PREPARATION NEEDED

- ❑ Photocopies of "What Gifts Do I Have?" on page 42, one per student
- ❑ Tape
- ❑ Pens or pencils

For leaders: We have provided a list of the gifts and their definitions at the end of this session.

WHAT GIFTS DO I HAVE?

Explain: **One of the greatest ways to identify our own gifts is to ask others. I'm giving you a copy of "What Gifts Do I Have?" Write your name at the top of the page and tape it to your back. Then I'm going to give us five minutes to walk around the room and approach each other and write down gifts that we think that person has on the "What Gifts Do I Have?" sheet that is taped on his/her back. For example, if you think Dave has the gift of teaching, you should write "teaching" on the "What Gifts Do I Have?" sheet on his back. If Kim has the gift of wisdom, you should write "wisdom" on her back. Let's begin!**

Ideally, your junior highers will stick to the gifts mentioned in 1 Corinthians 12, Romans 12 and Ephesians 4, but they might not be developmentally ready to identify these gifts in each other. If they seem to be struggling with this, expand the category of gifts to include talents such as great storyteller, or makes others feel welcome.

> **Tip:** You and/or your adult leadership team need to be aware of students who have few or no gifts written on their backs. Be sure to write a few gifts on their papers yourselves.

SESSION 2

After students have done this for several minutes, ask them to get into groups of four. Explain that one at a time, they should remove the sheets of paper from their backs and read what was written. Ask them to comment to their groups about whether or not what others wrote surprises them or if it's what they might have put themselves. Ask the group to help each person briefly discuss a few ways he or she could use that gift in the youth ministry, school, friendships or home.

Close by encouraging your students to keep these sheets as a reminder of not only their own unique gifts, but the importance of encouraging others to use their gifts.

ONE OF A KIND

▼▾▼▾▼▾▼▾▼▾▼▾▼▾▼▾▼▾▼

1. _____

2. _____   3. _____

4. _____

GIFTS GALORE

▼▼▼▼▼▼▼▼▼▼▼▼▼▼▼▼

Evangelizing

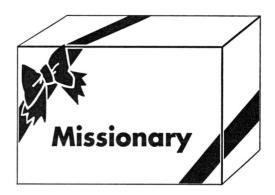

Missionary

Miracles

Giving

Teaching

Leadership

Serving

Healing

THE SPIRITUAL GIFTS DISCOVERY

▼▼▼▼▼▼▼▼▼▼▼

Evaluate each statement and decide how well it describes you on a scale of 0 to 3. If the sentence really describes you, write a 3 next to it. If it somewhat describes you, write a 2 next to it. If it describes you just a bit, write a 1 next to it. If it doesn't describe you at all, write a 0 next to it. Give yourself credit even if you tend to be shy and perhaps haven't tried something but feel you could have that gift.

_____ 1. I enjoy meeting the needs of others.

_____ 2. I receive joy doing the jobs that others see as lame.

_____ 3. I am very compassionate to people who need help.

_____ 4. I want my home to always be a spot where people in need can come, hang out and find rest.

_____ 5. I believe I have a prayer language which is a tongue unknown to me.

_____ 6. God has used me in a supernatural way to heal someone.

_____ 7. I have helped others in their struggles.

_____ 8. I try to use any money I get wisely and carefully.

_____ 9. I often see clear solutions to complicated problems.

_____ 10. I have helped others understand God's Word.

_____ 11. I find it easy to trust God in difficult situations.

_____ 12. I would like to be a missionary.

_____ 13. I am comfortable talking with nonbelievers about my relationship with Christ.

_____ 14. I have given others important messages that I felt came from God.

_____ 15. I enjoy understanding the Bible and explaining it to people.

_____ 16. I would like the responsibilities that my pastor and/or youth pastor have.

_____ 17. I believe I know where I am going and other people seem to follow me.

_____ 18. I can give others responsibilities for a task or project and then help them accomplish it.

_____ 19. Many incredible acts of God have happened to others through me.

_____ 20. There has been a time when I heard someone speak in an unknown language and I was able to interpret what he or she said.

_____ 21. I am the type of person who likes to reach out to needy people.

_____ 22. You will find me volunteering to do "behind the scenes" tasks that few notice but that must get done.

_____ 23. I would like to have a ministry with those who are needy.

_____ 24. I like having new friends in my home. I like making them feel comfortable.

_____ 25. I have spoken in tongues.

_____ 26. God has healed people after I have prayed for them.

_____ 27. I have helped others in their struggles.

_____ 28. I am a cheerful giver of my money.

_____ 29. God has given me the ability to give good advice to others.

_____ 30. I often learn new insights on my own as I read the Bible.

_____ 31. I am confident that God will come through in tough situations.

_____ 32. I have a strong desire to see people in other countries come to know Christ.

_____ 33. I always think of new ways in which I can share Christ with my non-Christian friends.

_____ 34. I desire to speak messages from God that will challenge people to change.

_____ 35. I think I may have what it takes to teach a Bible study or lead a small-group discussion.

_____ 36. I can see myself taking responsibility for the spiritual growth of others in my future.

_____ 37. When I'm in a group, I'm usually the leader or I take the lead if no one else does.

_____ 38. I am able to set goals and plans and I know how to get stuff done.

_____ 39. I have seen God's miracles in and through my life.

_____ 40. God has shown me what someone is saying when he or she is speaking in tongues.

MY OWN GIFTS

▼▼▼▼▼▼▼▼▼▼▼▼▼

In the spaces below, write the numbers of your responses to the statements from "The Spiritual Gifts Discovery" next to the corresponding number. For example, if you wrote a 3 next to statement 1, write a 3 next to the number 1 on this page.

Now add up the two numbers. Place the sum in the "Total" column.

Gifts	Value of Answers		Total
A. Serving	1 _____	21 _____	_____
B. Helping	2 _____	22 _____	_____
C. Mercy	3 _____	23 _____	_____
D. Hospitality	4 _____	24 _____	_____
E. Tongues	5 _____	25 _____	_____
F. Healing	6 _____	26 _____	_____
G. Exhortation	7 _____	27 _____	_____
H. Giving	8 _____	28 _____	_____
I. Wisdom	9 _____	29 _____	_____
J. Knowledge	10 _____	30 _____	_____
K. Faith	11 _____	31 _____	_____
L. Apostle/Missionary	12 _____	32 _____	_____
M. Evangelism	13 _____	33 _____	_____
N. Prophecy	14 _____	34 _____	_____
O. Teaching	15 _____	35 _____	_____
P. Pastoring	16 _____	36 _____	_____
Q. Leadership	17 _____	37 _____	_____
R. Administration	18 _____	38 _____	_____
S. Miracles	19 _____	39 _____	_____
T. Interpretation of Tongues	20 _____	40 _____	_____

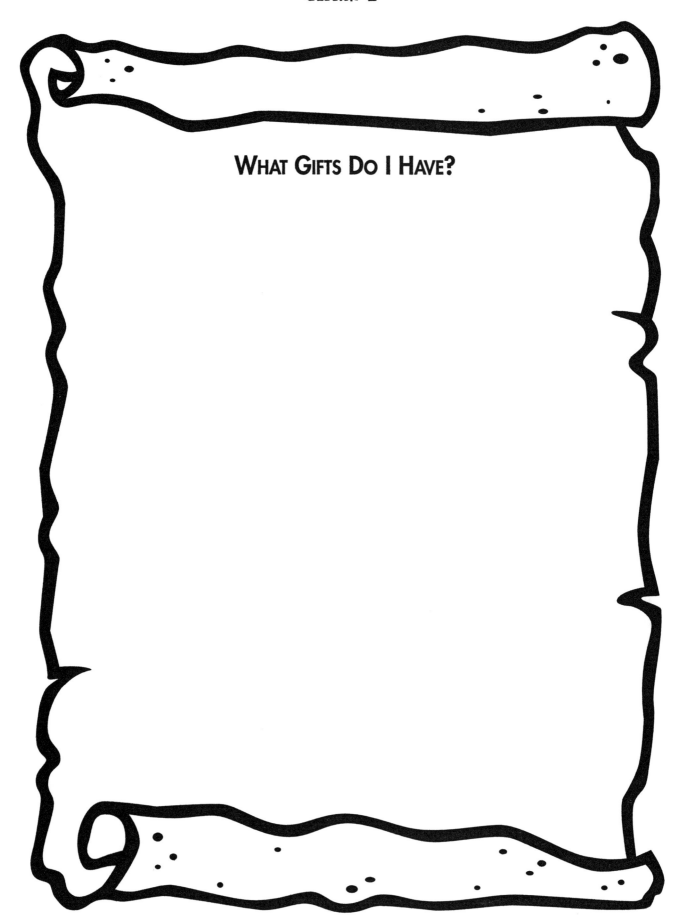

WHAT GIFTS DO I HAVE?

Please Note: This page is intended only for the leader's information and may not be photocopied. The leader may share the information to clarify the different gifts. For further information on spiritual gifts please refer to *Your Spiritual Gifts Can Help Your Church Grow* by C. Peter Wagner (Regal Books, 1994).

GIFT DEFINITIONS AND SCRIPTURE REFERENCES

▼▼▼▼▼▼▼▼▼▼▼▼▼▼

The following pages contain **suggested** definitions of the spiritual gifts. While not meant to be dogmatic or final, these definitions and supporting Scriptures do correspond to characteristics of the gifts as expressed in the *Wagner-Modified Houts Questionnaire*.[1]

A. **Prophecy.** The gift of prophecy is the special ability that God gives to certain members of the Body of Christ to receive and communicate an immediate message of God to His people through a divinely anointed utterance.

    Luke 7:26   Acts 15:32; 21:9-11
    Romans 12:6   1 Corinthians 12:10,28
    Ephesians 4:11-14

B. **Pastor.** The gift of pastor is the special ability that God gives to certain members of the Body of Christ to assume a long-term personal responsibility for the spiritual welfare of a group of believers.

    John 10:1-18   Ephesians 4:11-14
    1 Timothy 3:1-7   1 Peter 5:1-3

C. **Teaching.** The gift of teaching is the special ability that God gives to certain members of the Body of Christ to communicate information relevant to the health and ministry of the Body and its members in such a way that others will learn.

    Acts 18:24-28; 20:20,21   Romans 12:7
    1 Corinthians 12:28   Ephesians 4:11-14

D. Wisdom. The gift of wisdom is the special ability that God gives to certain members of the Body of Christ to know the mind of the Holy Spirit in such a way as to receive insight into how given knowledge may best be applied to specific needs arising in the Body of Christ.

Acts 6:3,10	1 Corinthians 2:1-13; 12:8
James 1:5,6	2 Peter 3:15,16

E. Knowledge. The gift of knowledge is the special ability that God gives to certain members of the Body of Christ to discover, accumulate, analyze and clarify information and ideas which are pertinent to the well-being of the Body.

Acts 5:1-11	1 Corinthians 2:14; 12:8
2 Corinthians 11:6	Colossians 2:2,3

F. Exhortation. The gift of exhortation is the special ability that God gives to certain members of the Body of Christ to minister words of comfort, consolation, encouragement and counsel to other members of the Body in such a way that they feel helped and healed.

Acts 14:22	Romans 12:8
1 Timothy 4:13	Hebrews 10:25

G. Discerning of Spirits. The gift of discerning of spirits is the special ability that God gives to certain members of the Body of Christ to know with assurance whether certain behavior purported to be of God is in reality divine, human or satanic.

Matthew 16:21-23	Acts 5:1-11; 16:16-18
1 Corinthians 12:10	1 John 4:1-6

H. Giving. The gift of giving is the special ability that God gives to certain members of the Body of Christ to contribute their material resources to the work of the Lord with liberality and cheerfulness.

Mark 12:41-44	Romans 12:8
2 Corinthians 8:1-7; 9:2-8	

I. Helps. The gift of helps is the special ability that God gives to certain members of the Body of Christ to invest the talents they have in the life and ministry of other members of the Body, thus enabling those others to increase the effectiveness of their own spiritual gifts.

    Mark 15:40,41   Luke 8:2,3
    Acts 9:36   Romans 16:1,2
    1 Corinthians 12:28

J. Mercy. The gift of mercy is the special ability that God gives to certain members of the Body of Christ to feel genuine empathy and compassion for individuals (both Christian and non-Christian) who suffer distressing physical, mental or emotional problems, and to translate that compassion into cheerfully done deeds which reflect Christ's love and alleviate the suffering.

    Matthew 20:29-34; 25:34-40   Mark 9:41
    Luke 10:33-35   Acts 11:28-30; 16:33,34
    Romans 12:8

K. Missionary. The gift of missionary is the special ability that God gives to certain members of the Body of Christ to minister whatever other spiritual gifts they have in a second culture.

    Acts 8:4; 13:2,3; 22:21   Romans 10:15
    1 Corinthians 9:19-23

L. Evangelist. The gift of evangelist is the special ability that God gives to certain members of the Body of Christ to share the gospel with unbelievers in such a way that men and women become Jesus' disciples and responsible members of the Body of Christ.

    Acts 8:5,6,26-40; 14:21; 21:8   Ephesians 4:11-14
    2 Timothy 4:5

M. Hospitality. The gift of hospitality is the special ability that God gives to certain members of the Body of Christ to provide an open house and a warm welcome to those in need of food and lodging.

    Acts 16:14,15   Romans 12:9-13; 16:23
    Hebrews 13:1,2   1 Peter 4:9

N. Faith. The gift of faith is the special ability that God gives to certain members of the Body of Christ to discern with extraordinary confidence the will and purposes of God for His work.

    Acts 11:22-24; 27:21-25   Romans 4:18-21
    1 Corinthians 12:9   Hebrews 11

O. Leadership. The gift of leadership is the special ability that God gives to certain members of the Body of Christ to set goals in accordance with God's purpose for the future and to communicate these goals to others in such a way that they voluntarily and harmoniously work together to accomplish those goals for the glory of God.

    Luke 9:51   Acts 7:10; 15:7-11
    Romans 12:8   1 Timothy 5:17
    Hebrews 13:17

P. Administration. The gift of administration is the special ability that God gives to certain members of the Body of Christ to understand clearly the immediate and long-range goals of a particular unit of the Body of Christ and to devise and execute effective plans for the accomplishment of those goals.

    Luke 14:28-30   Acts 6:1-7; 27:11
    1 Corinthians 12:28   Titus 1:5

Q. Miracles. The gift of miracles is the special ability that God gives to certain members of the Body of Christ to serve as human intermediaries through whom it pleases God to perform powerful acts that are perceived by observers to have altered the ordinary course of nature.

    Acts 9:36-42; 19:11-20; 20:7-12   Romans 15:18,19
    1 Corinthians 12:10,28   2 Corinthians 12:12

R. Healing. The gift of healing is the special ability that God gives to certain members of the Body of Christ to serve as human intermediaries through whom it pleases God to cure illness and restore health apart from the use of natural means.

    Acts 3:1-10; 5:12-16; 9:32-35; 28:7-10
    1 Corinthians 12:9,28

S. Tongues. The gift of tongues is the special ability that God gives to certain members of the Body of Christ (a) to speak to God in a language they have never learned and/or (b) to receive and communicate an immediate message of God to His people through a divinely anointed utterance in a language they never learned.

    Mark 16:17   Acts 2:1-13; 10:44-46; 19:1-7
    1 Corinthians 12:10,28; 14:13-19

T. Interpretation. The gift of interpretation is the special ability that God gives to certain members of the Body of Christ to make known in the vernacular the message of one who speaks in tongues.

    1 Corinthians 12:10,30; 14:13; 14:26-28

U. Voluntary Poverty. The gift of voluntary poverty is the special ability that God gives to certain members of the Body of Christ to renounce material comfort and luxury and adopt a personal lifestyle equivalent to those living at the poverty level in a given society in order to serve God more effectively.

    Acts 2:44,45; 4:34-37   1 Corinthians 13:1-3
    2 Corinthians 6:10; 8:9

V. Celibacy. The gift of celibacy is the special ability that God gives to certain members of the Body of Christ to remain single and enjoy it; to be unmarried and not suffer undue sexual temptations.

    Matthew 19:10-12   1 Corinthians 7:7,8

SESSION 2

W. Intercession. The gift of intercession is the special ability that God gives to certain members of the Body of Christ to pray for extended periods of time on a regular basis and see frequent and specific answers to their prayers, to a degree much greater than that which is expected of the average Christian.

Luke 22:41-44   Acts 12:12

Colossians 1:9-12; 4:12,13   1 Timothy 2:1,2

James 5:14-16

X. Exorcism. The gift of exorcism is the special ability that God gives to certain members of the Body of Christ to cast out demons and evil spirits.

Matthew 12:22-32   Luke 10:12-20

Acts 8:5-8; 16:16-18

Y. Service. The gift of service is the special ability that God gives to certain members of the Body of Christ to identify the unmet needs involved in a task related to God's work, and to make use of available resources to meet those needs and help accomplish the desired results.

Acts 6:1-7   Romans 12:7

Galatians 6:2,10   2 Timothy 1:16-18

Titus 3:14

Note:

1. Taken from C. Peter Wagner, *Your Spiritual Gifts Can Help Your Church Grow Study Guide* (Ventura, Calif.: Gospel Light, 1995), pp. 111-117.

UP AND OUT

LEADER'S DEVOTIONAL

You can't believe what you've just heard. Your favorite contemporary Christian singer has just been caught in adultery. He has confessed that last year a beautiful woman walked backstage after a concert. With his wife back home, he couldn't resist the chance to take this woman out for coffee. One thing led to another, and they spent the night together.

Now that this singer has spent several months in counseling and repentance, he wants to return to concert ministry. Has he forever ruined the musical gifts that God has given him or will God be able to use his amazing singing voice again?

Before you answer that question, you may want to think about the Old Testament example of David. David, although a great leader, made the same kind of mistakes that the famous singer had. After all, even after we are saved by Christ, we are still tempted by sin.

And yet in the midst of our sin and our humanity, God uses us. As you study Matthew 22:34-39, 1 Samuel 16:14-23 and Psalm 9:1,2 with your students, please keep in mind the true story of David—a man after God's own heart who also possessed incredible musical gifts—but nonetheless, a man. Just like David, your students can use their abilities to praise God and serve others in the midst of their sin, weakness and timidity.

KEY VERSES

"One of them, an expert in the law, tested him with this question: 'Teacher, which is the greatest commandment in the Law?' Jesus replied: 'Love the Lord your God with all your heart and with all your soul and with all your mind. This is the first and greatest commandment. And the second is like it: Love your neighbor as yourself.'" Matthew 22:35-39

BIBLICAL BASIS

1 Samuel 16:14-23; Psalm 9:1,2; Matthew 22:34-39; Romans 12:4-8; 1 Corinthians 12:1-11; Ephesians 4:11,12

FOCUS OF THIS SESSION

We can use our abilities to praise God and to serve others.

AIMS OF THIS SESSION

During this session students will:
- Discover the two most important rules in all of Scripture;
- Realize that the two primary uses of their talents are to praise God and to serve others;
- Identify several real-life ways they can use their abilities to praise God and to serve others.

APPROACH THE WORD

(15 MINUTES)

OBJECTIVE

To help students realize the importance of clear and consistent rules.

MATERIALS AND PREPARATION NEEDED

- ❏ 50 green balloons
- ❏ 50 blue balloons
- ❏ 50 red balloons
- ❏ Several large trash bags
- ❏ Upbeat music and player

Ahead of time, inflate all the colored balloons.

DON'T CHANGE THE RULES!

Be sure to welcome students as they enter the room. To begin the lesson, explain: **Today we've got a "boys against girls" competition. I need all the boys on the left side of the room and all of the girls on the right side of the room.** If at all possible, have students remove their shoes. Place all of the colored balloons in the middle of the floor between the two groups as you continue to explain: **I'm going to give each side a trash bag, and your goal is to pick up as many balloons as you can with your feet and walk or kick them over to your team's trash bag. Once you get right next to the trash bag, you can pick them up with your hands to put them in the bag. But that is the only time you can use your hands.** Depending on how big the balloons are you may need more than one trash bag.

Explain: **Here is how we will score the game. The green balloons are worth fifty points. The blue balloons are worth twenty points and the red balloons are worth ten points. If at any time you want to get rid of some balloons from your bag, you're welcome to throw them back into the center of the room. Ready? Go for it!** You may want to play upbeat background music to help create a lively atmosphere.

After one or two minutes, yell: **Wait a minute. The rules have changed. Now the green balloons are negative ten points, the blue balloons are worth thirty points and the red balloons are worth fifty points.** If students complain, explain that rules sometimes change and they'll just have to adjust. After another minute or two, yell: **Whoops! Rules have changed again. Now the green balloons are worth 100 points, the blue balloons are negative ten points and the red balloons are worth zero points.**

After another two minutes, stop the game. Have a few adult volunteers tabulate the scores given the third set of rules and then declare a winning team. Discuss with the group:

How did it feel when I kept changing the rules?
Why are rules important?
What are the best kind of rules?

Transition to the rest of the lesson by explaining: **Today we're going to examine the two most important rules in the whole world.**

BIBLE EXPLORATION

(35 MINUTES)

OBJECTIVE

To define for students the two most important rules in Scripture and apply them to their spiritual gifts.

MATERIALS AND PREPARATION NEEDED

- ❏ White board, chalkboard or overhead projector and transparency and pens or chalk
- ❏ Felt-tip pens
- ❏ Four large sheets of poster paper
- ❏ Tape

THE UNCHANGEABLE RULES

Ask your junior highers: **Where can we find a list of the most important rules in the whole world?** Once students guess the Bible, ask: **What are some of the rules that Scripture mentions?** Make a list of these rules on the white board, chalkboard or overhead. After several minutes, ask students to vote on what they think are the most important rules. They will likely choose rules such as no adultery, no lying, no killing, etc.

Explain: **Let's see what Scripture itself has to say.** Ask for a volunteer to read Matthew 22:34-39, then discuss: **What are the two most important rules that Jesus mentions? How close were we to getting these two most important rules?**

The amazing truth is that all of the other rules we've already mentioned somehow relate to either loving God or loving others. Let's go back through our earlier list and decide together whether each rule relates to loving God, loving others, or both.

Once you have finished this exercise, ask: **How do these two rules relate to spiritual gifts? They show us the goal of our spiritual gifts: to praise God and serve others. It's not to look good, be popular or be cool.**

Have students return to the guys' group and the girls' group. In front of each group, tape two pieces of poster board to the walls. Write "God" on the left poster board of each team and "Others" on the right poster board of each team. Explain: **We're going to do a tag team game. I'm going to call out either "God" or "Others." When you hear that, one volunteer from each side should run up to the corresponding piece of poster board and write one way to use our talents and spiritual gifts to praise God or serve others, depending on which category I call out.** (*Note:* Before you begin, you may want to do a brief five-minute review of your last session to remind students of some of the spiritual gifts described in 1 Corinthians 12:1-11; Romans 12:4-8 and Ephesians 4:11,12.) **Once the first volunteer writes one way to serve on either the "God" or "Others" poster board, return to your team and hand your pen to someone else who has another way to serve God or others. Your team is to keep focusing on the first category I call out until I say the second category. For example, if I start by calling "God," then you keep writing ways to serve God with those gifts and talents until I yell "Others." Keep passing the pen to other team members so everyone gets to be involved.**

Give the group 7 to 10 minutes as you keep yelling either "God" or "Others." At the end, ask: **How similar are the "God" and "Others" lists?** Chances are that they will be pretty similar, so explain: **Serving God and serving others go hand in hand. Obeying Jesus' first rule with your talents means you will probably be obeying His second rule at the same time.**

At this point, tape the poster board to the wall in a cross formation by placing the two sheets labeled "God," one on top of the other, as the vertical half of the cross and the two pieces labeled "Others," on either side of the "God" sheets, as the horizontal half of the cross. Explain: **The cross represents our desire to follow Christ in everything we do. In using our spiritual gifts, praising God and serving others cannot be separated. Although we usually think of praising God as singing songs, we praise God also by the way that we use our gifts.**

SESSION 3

Note: If you are completing this session in one meeting, ignore this break and skip to "Conclusion and Decision."

Two-Meeting Track: If you want to spread this session over two meetings, STOP here and close in prayer. Inform students of the content to be covered in your next meeting.

APPROACH THE WORD

(15 MINUTES)

OBJECTIVE

To trigger students' memories about the two important goals of praising God and serving others.

MATERIALS AND PREPARATION NEEDED

☐ White board, chalkboard or overhead projector and transparency and pens or chalk

WHAT ARE YOU DOING?

Begin by asking for two volunteers to play this hilarious game. Explain that the first student begins by pantomiming an action, such as riding a bike, stirring cake batter, climbing a tree or walking a dog. After a few seconds of this pantomime, the second student asks the first, "What are you doing?" At that point, the first student gives an answer OTHER THAN what they are actually doing. For instance, if the first student is riding a bike, the second student asks, "What are you doing?" and the first student responds with something such as, "Skipping rope." At that point, the second student has to pretend to skip rope. After a few seconds, the first student, who is still pretending to ride a bike, asks, "What are you doing?" The second student responds with something like, "Playing soccer," at which point the first student who has been riding a bike begins to play soccer.

From this point on, the first and second students alternate asking and answering the question, "What are you doing?" A student is eliminated if he doesn't have an immediate answer to the question, "What are you doing?" Once a student is eliminated, ask for another volunteer to take that place and the game continues. Repeat this process for approximately eight minutes.

Ask your junior highers: **What were some of the actions you remember students doing?** Make a list of their answers on the white board, chalkboard or overhead. Randomly point to one response at a time and ask either: **How can you use this activity to praise God? Or, How can you use this activity to serve others?** After you have pointed to 5 to 10 different activities from the game and brainstormed how to use this activity to serve God or others, ask: **Were there any activities in this game that cannot be used to serve God or others?** The answer to this question is a definite no, so if students suggest an activity, challenge students to find a creative use for any activity, regardless of how random or bizarre it is.

Transition to the rest of the lesson by explaining: **Today we are going to study a well-known leader in the Bible who knew what it meant to use every activity to serve God or others.**

BIBLE EXPLORATION TWO

▼▼▼▼▼▼▼▼▼▼▼▼

(30 MINUTES)

OBJECTIVE

To help students put themselves in the position of David and understand his commitment to using his gifts to serve God and others.

MATERIALS AND PREPARATION NEEDED

❑ Photocopy one copy of "Melodrama Madness" on page 58
❑ White board, chalkboard or overhead projector and transparency and pens or chalk

MELODRAMA MADNESS

Ask: **How many of you have heard of David in the Bible? What do you know about him?** Your students' answers will probably focus on his

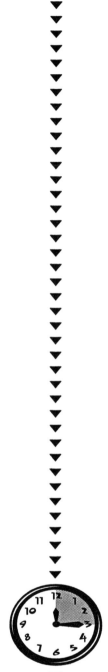

defeat of Goliath and his adultery with Bathsheba. Explain: **It just goes to show you that in most ways, David was just like us. He had some good days, such as when he beat Goliath, and he had some bad days, such as when he committed adultery with Bathsheba.**

In the midst of the good and the bad, David remained a man after God's own heart. That's because he used his gifts to serve God and others. Today we are going to act out the story of David right out of 1 Samuel 16:14-23 and Psalm 9:1,2. I need eight volunteers to help me.

Once you have your eight volunteers, assign each one a role from the "Melodrama Madness" resource. Ask each of your actors to be as animated as possible, and ask the rest of your students to be sure to cheer on the actors.

After you have finished the "Melodrama Madness," discuss: **Put yourself in David's position as a teenager coming before the king. What obstacles might have prevented David from using his gifts?** Answers may include he felt too young, he was intimidated by the king, he was insecure.

At this point, share an example from your own life about your struggles with serving God and others. You may want to highlight specific obstacles such as feelings of inadequacy, fears of rejection, lack of time.

Ask your students: **What are some of the things that keep you from being like David and using your gifts to serve God and others?** Make a list of these obstacles on the white board, and then discuss one obstacle at a time. Ask: **How can we overcome this obstacle?**

CONCLUSION AND DECISION

(15 MINUTES)

OBJECTIVE

To help students overcome any obstacles that prevent them from using their gifts by finding an immediate opportunity to serve God and others.

MATERIALS AND PREPARATION NEEDED

❑ Photocopy of "Right Away" on page 59, one copy for every four students
❑ Pencils
❑ Prizes for the winning team

RIGHT AWAY

Explain: **One of the main ways to overcome these obstacles to serving God and others is simply to get moving and try it. I want you to get into groups of four.** Once they are in groups of four, distribute a copy of "Right Away" and one pencil for each group and explain: **Your goal as a team is to walk around the church (or block, neighborhood or school, depending on your setting) and look for ways that you could use a skill or ability, or simply your time, to serve God or others. For example, you might realize that the parking lot needs painting, bathrooms need cleaning or parents need help getting their children to their classrooms. Using this handout, choose someone in your group to write down anything you could do** *right away* **to serve God and others. You will receive 1,000 points for every idea you have when you return. If you actually have the time to complete the action, please do so. Then circle that activity on your "Right Away" sheet, and you will receive 5,000 points when you return. You have fifteen minutes to work together, and the winning group will receive a prize.** You should make sure that everyone is clear on the exact time to return before you send them on their way.

After the groups return, ask an adult volunteer to tally up the scores as you lead a discussion by asking:

What activities did you actually get to do?

What other ideas did you think of?

Now you've seen that most obstacles can be overcome, often by simply getting started. Close in prayer, asking God to help you and your students overcome the obstacles that prevent them from serving God and others.

MELODRAMA MADNESS

▼▼▼▼▼▼▼▼▼▼▼▼▼

BASED ON 1 SAMUEL 16:14-23

You play the part of the narrator. You set the tone, so please read the narration with a very lively and animated tone. Instruct the "actors" to dive into their parts with gusto. Ask the audience to cheer on the actors. Be sure to pause and allow the actors to perform their actions.

To act out this melodrama, you will need eight volunteers to play the following parts:

Characters

Saul

Two servants

Jesse

Donkey

Loaf of bread

David

The harp (makes "music" when David is "playing" it)

Once there was a powerful king named Saul. For a while, the Spirit of the Lord was on Saul and God worked mightily through him.

But then Saul grew proud. When he walked around the kingdom, he walked with a cocky attitude.

Every night Saul would go to bed, and he would snore loudly. Very loudly. Yet he would wake up in the middle of the night screaming. This was because an evil spirit was tormenting him.

Two of Saul's servants came to him on their knees. They said together, "You need someone to play the harp for you to make you feel better."

Saul sat up and yelled (why he was yelling, we don't know), "You're absolutely right. Find me someone."

The tallest of Saul's servants yelled back, "Okey dokey. How about David?"

Saul yelled back, "Sounds great."

Saul's two servants were so excited that Saul liked their idea that they skipped out of the room.

The two servants ran all the way to David's house. His house was far away so they had to keep running.

They told David's father, Jesse, what Saul wanted and Jesse told David, "You must go with these two servants." He put David and a loaf of bread on top of a donkey and sent them back to Saul.

When David reached Saul, he skipped and sang, "I'm so happy to be here. I'm so happy to be here." And then David began to play his harp and sing, "I will praise you, O God."

(Note to narrator: Make sure to have the harp make some noises while David makes up his own song.) And the harp was making beautiful music.

Saul sang back, "I'm so happy that you're here."

David kept singing. The harp kept making its noise. Saul kept singing.

Saul went back to bed and snored loudly, for David's harp playing had calmed him.

The End

RIGHT AWAY

▼▾▼▾▼▾▼▾▼▾▼▾▼▾▼▾▼▾▼

Using this handout, write down anything you could do *right away* to serve God and others. You will receive 1,000 points for every idea you have when you return.

If you actually have the time to complete the action, please do so. Then *circle that activity on this sheet*, and you will receive 5,000 points when you return. You have twenty minutes to work together, and the winning group will receive a prize.

NEEDING THE KNEE

LEADER'S DEVOTIONAL

Think about your students for a moment. Picture a few of their faces. Remember several of their names. Reflect on what spiritual gifts they might have. Who among them has the gift of mercy? Who has the gift of teaching? Service? Prophecy? Giving?

The truth is *they all do*. Well, none of them individually has all the gifts, but as a part of the Body of Christ, they all have access to the gifts.

This session is going to ask students to work together to develop their gifts. For some it will come naturally. For others it will be a challenge. Your job is to help them work together even as they are learning together. That means no sarcasm, no biting jokes and no competitive comments.

Once again think about your students. Picture what your ministry would look like if they acted as if they were all on the same team, working together, praying together and serving together. Now picture what your city would be like if all this were happening. It would be a different place, wouldn't it?

Working and praying together, you and your students can accomplish anything God calls you to do.

Working separately, you and your students are set on a path of loneliness, frustration and disappointment. After all, there is no such thing as a Lone Ranger Christian. Even the Lone Ranger had Tonto!

SESSION 4

KEY VERSES

"But in fact God has arranged the parts in the body, every one of them, just as he wanted them to be. If they were all one part, where would the body be? As it is, there are many parts, but one body." 1 Corinthians 12:18-20

BIBLICAL BASIS

1 Corinthians 12:12-31; Ephesians 2:10

FOCUS OF THIS SESSION

We can use our unique talents as we work together in God's family.

AIMS OF THIS SESSION

During this session students will:
- Examine the command of 1 Corinthians 12 to be united and cooperate in the midst of their diversity;
- Discover the advantages of working together in the Body;
- Identify one person they can encourage today.

APPROACH THE WORD

(25 MINUTES)

OBJECTIVE

To drive home to your students the need for cooperation and teamwork.

MATERIALS AND PREPARATION NEEDED

- ☐ One (or more) copies of "Team Obstacle Course" on pages 70-71

❑ Scissors or paper cutter

❑ A large sheet of poster board

❑ Felt-tip pens

Ahead of time, cut the "Team Obstacle Course" resource along its dotted lines to form 12 strips of paper, each with its own instruction. Make sure you have one strip of paper per student expected, which may mean making more copies of "Team Obstacle Course." Being creative with your meeting space, you should also select an obstacle course that will take approximately seven minutes to complete. It should include several tricky tasks, such as crawling under a desk, circling a tree, and walking down a staircase. It's best if you diagram this obstacle course ahead of time on a large sheet of poster board so that students have a visual aid to help them remember the course.

TEAM OBSTACLE COURSE

Be sure to greet your students warmly and explain: **We have a special start for today's lesson. We're going to do an obstacle course together.** Explain the course with the diagram and continue: **The goal is not to win, but to have everyone complete the obstacle course. There is one trick, though. Each of you has a special role to play in the obstacle course.** At this point, distribute the strips with instructions and ask students not to tell anyone about their role but to walk normally toward the beginning of the obstacle course. You may want to distribute these strips strategically and give the instructions to be mute to the more verbal and commanding students and the instructions to make unhelpful suggestions to your most creative and humorous students. Once you reach the beginning of the obstacle course, explain: **Now you should start playing your part. Remember the goal is to complete the course, not to win. I'll walk ahead of all of you on the course to make sure you are heading in the right direction.**

What tends to happen during this exercise is that some students try on their own to complete the course while others try to work together. Either way, students will inevitably be amused with the exercise.

Once everyone has completed the course and you have gathered back together, discuss the following questions: **What went well in this obstacle course? Looking back, what do you think you should have done differently? What does this say about teamwork? Today we're going to look at how much we can get done with teamwork. We'll see there's no obstacle we can't overcome if we work together.**

SESSION 4

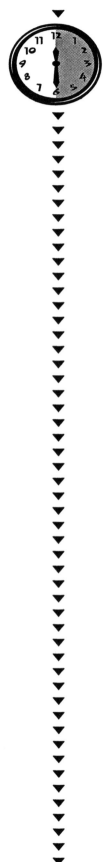

BIBLE EXPLORATION

(30 MINUTES)

OBJECTIVE

To integrate Paul's teachings about teamwork into students' thinking about spiritual gifts.

MATERIALS AND PREPARATION NEEDED

- ❏ One copy of "Crisis Counseling Center" on page 72
- ❏ Copies of "Your Counseling Manual" on page 73, one per every four students
- ❏ Envelopes
- ❏ Paper
- ❏ Pens or pencils
- ❏ A tape recorder
- ❏ Option: A food prize for the winners (i.e., candy, popsicle, etc.)

Ahead of time, ask a male and a female student to read and record the parts of Marco and Linda on a tape recorder. Make sure they have practiced in advance so that their voices are clear and smooth.

Also, make enough copies of "Your Counseling Manual" so that there is one for every four students and cut it along the lines indicated so that it is divided into different puzzle pieces. Mix up all of the pieces and then divide the random pieces into the same number of envelopes as you made copies of "Your Counseling Manual" (one per four students).

TEAMWORK

Explain: **Today we are going to learn a lot about using our talents for working together as a team. I want you to get into groups of four students each.** Once they have done this, explain: **Each group of four students is now a special crisis counseling center. Every day you are visited by all sorts of students with all types of problems, such as being a victim of gossip, failing in math class, or fighting with parents or stepparents. Today you have two very special clients. Listen to the first one.**

Play the prerecorded tape of the student reading the part of Marco. Stop the tape, distribute paper and pens or pencils to each group and ask: **How would you help Marco? What would you say to him? What would you recommend that he do? Work together as a team and write down your advice.**

After giving them five minutes to respond to Marco, ask for a few groups to volunteer to share their advice for him. Then explain: **OK, now we've got a second student who has dropped into your counseling center. Her name is Linda and she needs your help.** Play the tape of Linda and then ask: **How would you help Linda? What would you say to her? What would you recommend that she do? Work together as a team and write down your advice.**

After giving them five minutes to respond to Linda, ask for the groups to volunteer to share their advice to her. Then explain: **Actually, you have a special counseling manual that is going to help you give Marco and Linda the advice they need.** Pass out one of the envelopes to each group and explain: **Here are some puzzle pieces of your manual. The trick is that there is not a complete puzzle here. You are going to have to walk around from group to group and trade pieces to get all the pieces that you need.**

Note: You may want to make it more competitive by having a food prize for the group that completes their puzzle first.

Once each group has completed its puzzle, have someone read it aloud for the whole group. Then explain: **Scripture is *always* the best guidebook, no matter what our problem or situation may be. How does this make a difference in the advice you would give Marco or Linda? What would you add to what you have already written? What would you subtract?**

Note: If you are completing this session in one meeting, ignore this break and skip to "Conclusion and Decision."

Two-Meeting Track: If you want to spread this session over two meetings, STOP here and close in prayer. Inform students of the content to be covered in your next meeting.

SESSION 4

REVIEW AND APPROACH

(15 MINUTES)

OBJECTIVE

To remind students of the importance of working together as a team, even when it is challenging.

MATERIALS AND PREPARATION NEEDED

❑ Three chairs facing the audience

MR. KNOW-IT-ALL

Begin the session by explaining: **We're going to play a game called "Mr. Know-It-All." I need three volunteers.** Once you have three volunteers, ask them to sit in the three chairs and explain: **You three combine to form the immense brain of "Mr. Know-It-All." You will take questions from the audience and answer them together without consulting ahead of time. The way you answer is by giving one word each. For example, the person in chair one might say "the." The person in chair two might add, "best." The person in chair three might add, "answer." Then we return to the person in chair one who would add, "to," chair two would add, "your," chair three would add, "question" and so on until they actually complete a sentence and hopefully give a coherent answer to the question.** Instruct the audience that questions should be outrageous, such as: **How would a pregnant cow get to the moon? Or: Why does the alphabet have 26 letters?**

After each question has been answered, ask for three new volunteers from the audience. Continue this for 8 or 10 minutes or until students start to lose interest. Then discuss:
What is the key to success for Mr. Know-It-All?
Why is it tough to work together?
Since it's tough, why try at all?

BIBLE EXPLORATION TWO

▼▾▼▾▼▾▼▾▼▾▼▾▼

(30 MINUTES)

OBJECTIVE

To give students real-life examples of people who are using their gifts for God's purposes.

MATERIALS AND PREPARATION NEEDED

- ❑ Four chairs
- ❑ Make an overhead transparency (or photocopies, one for each student) of "The Scoop from Paul" on page 74
- ❑ An overhead projector

Ahead of time, select four people from your church to serve on "The Gifts Panel." They should be people who possess strong verbal skills, a commitment to using their gifts, and an appreciation for junior highers. Try to get panel members of diverse gender, age, backgrounds and gifts. Explain that you would like them to serve on a "Gifts Panel" to share the ways they are using their gifts. It's best if you have one or two junior highers actually emcee the panel, which means preparing them ahead of time.

Beforehand, brainstorm questions with your student emcee(s) that they can ask panel members, such as: What are your gifts? When did you first start using your spiritual gifts? What is the best thing about trying to use your spiritual gifts? How have others helped you learn to use your gifts? Do you ever feel like you just want to quit using your gifts to serve others? What advice would you give a junior higher who isn't sure if he or she has any gifts at all?

THE GIFTS PANEL

Explain to the class: **The Bible is a very alive book, but we're not always sure how to make it alive in our own lives.** Put the overhead of "The Scoop from Paul" on the overhead projector (or give each student a copy) and continue: **Today we're going to look at Ephesians 2:10 where Paul wrote, "For we are God's workmanship, created in Christ Jesus to do good works, which God prepared in advance for** us to do." We have several guests today who are going to help us learn how to put this verse into action.

Introduce your four panel members and your student emcee(s). It's best to begin with a few prepared questions and then ask if your students have any questions to add. Leave the Ephesians 2:10 overhead on as a reminder of the theme of this session. Make sure the last question is something like: **How have others encouraged you to use your gifts for good works?**

CONCLUSION AND DECISION

(15 MINUTES)

OBJECTIVE

To help students identify another person they can encourage today.

MATERIALS AND PREPARATION NEEDED

- ❑ Photocopy "Special Delivery Mail" on page 75, one for each student
- ❑ Envelopes
- ❑ Pens or pencils

SPECIAL DELIVERY ENCOURAGEMENT

Explain: **We need other people to encourage us to use our gifts. To encourage means to put courage into. And we have the chance to be used by God to encourage others. I'm going to give you a copy of "Special Delivery Mail" and I want you to write a letter to someone who isn't here today who you think needs some courage put into them. It may be your teacher, your friend or your grandparent. Make sure the focus of your letter is the gifts and abilities you have seen in them and how you know God has great things ahead for them.**

Give students envelopes so that they can put their "Special Delivery Mail" letter in them, hopefully making it easier for them to mail once they get home. Or if they are writing someone from your church, you can offer to collect the envelopes, locate the addresses and mail them yourself.

Bring all the envelopes to the front of the room, and ask a few students to close in prayer, requesting that God use these letters to put courage into friends and family members.

TEAM OBSTACLE COURSE

▼▾▼▾▼▾▼▾▼▾▼▾▼▾▼▾▼

You are mute.

You are mute.

You are mute.

You are well intentioned and trying to help, but your frequent suggestions mislead and hinder progress.

You have to put your hands behind your back or in your pockets because you can't use them.

You have no use of one arm (choose which one).

You have no use of your arms and legs at all.

You have stiff elbows and knees. You cannot bend them at all.

You have stiff elbows and knees. You cannot bend them at all.

You are blind.

You have use of only one leg. You can switch back and forth if your one good leg gets tired.

CRISIS COUNSELING CENTER
▼▾▼▾▼▾▼▾▼▾▼▾▼▾▼

MARCO'S STORY

(Should be read with a self-pitying and sad voice.)

"I'm no good at anything. In math class, I'm always the one with the lowest grade. In basketball, I'm always the last one picked when they choose teams. My best friend just moved away and now I don't even have anyone to sit with at lunch. Even at home, my big brother gets all the attention now that he got into the state college and got a full-ride scholarship in tennis. I'll never be as good as he is, no matter how hard I try."

LINDA'S STORY

(Should be read with a bratty, snobby voice!)

"Tasha is sooooo jealous of me. She wanted to be on the school cheerleading squad, but I beat her in the competition. She liked Carl and Carl was interested in her for a while, but yesterday Carl asked to sit next to me at lunch, not her. Even in history, her best subject, I just won first place at the history fair and she only won third. I tried to be nice to her yesterday, but when the woman down the street asked me to baby-sit her two kids this Friday instead of Tasha, Tasha got really ticked off. I know Tasha will be glaring at me all through science class tomorrow, but I can't help it if I keep beating her in the stuff we do together."

YOUR COUNSELING MANUAL
▼▽▼▽▼▽▼▽▼▽▼▽▼▽

The body is a unit, though it is made up of many parts; and though all its parts are many, they form one body. So it is with Christ. For we were all baptized by one Spirit into one body—whether Jews or Greeks, slave or free—and we were all given the one Spirit to drink.

Now the body is not made up of one part but of many. If the foot should say, "Because I am not a hand, I do not belong to the body," it would not for that reason cease to be part of the body. And if the ear should say, "Because I am not an eye, I do not belong to the body," it would not for that reason cease to be part of the body. If the whole body were an eye, where would the sense of hearing be? If the whole body were an ear, where would the sense of smell be? But in fact God has arranged the parts in the body, every one of them, just as he wanted them to be. If they were all one part, where would the body be? As it is, there are many parts, but one body.

The eye cannot say to the hand, "I don't need you!" And the head cannot say to the feet, "I don't need you!" On the contrary, those parts of the body that seem to be weaker are indispensable, and the parts that we think are less honorable we treat with special honor. And the parts that are unpresentable are treated with special modesty, while our presentable parts need no special treatment. But God has combined the members of the body and has given greater honor to the parts that lacked it, so that there should be no division in the body, but that its parts should have equal concern for each other. If one part suffers, every part suffers with it; if one part is honored, every part rejoices with it.

Now you are the body of Christ, and each one of you is a part of it. And in the church God has appointed first of all apostles, second prophets, third teachers, then workers of miracles, also those having gifts of healing, those able to help others, those with gifts of administration, and those speaking in different kinds of tongues. Are all apostles? Are all prophets? Are all teachers? Do all work miracles? Do all have gifts of healing? Do all speak in tongues? Do all interpret? But eagerly desire the greater gifts.

—1 Corinthians 12:12-31

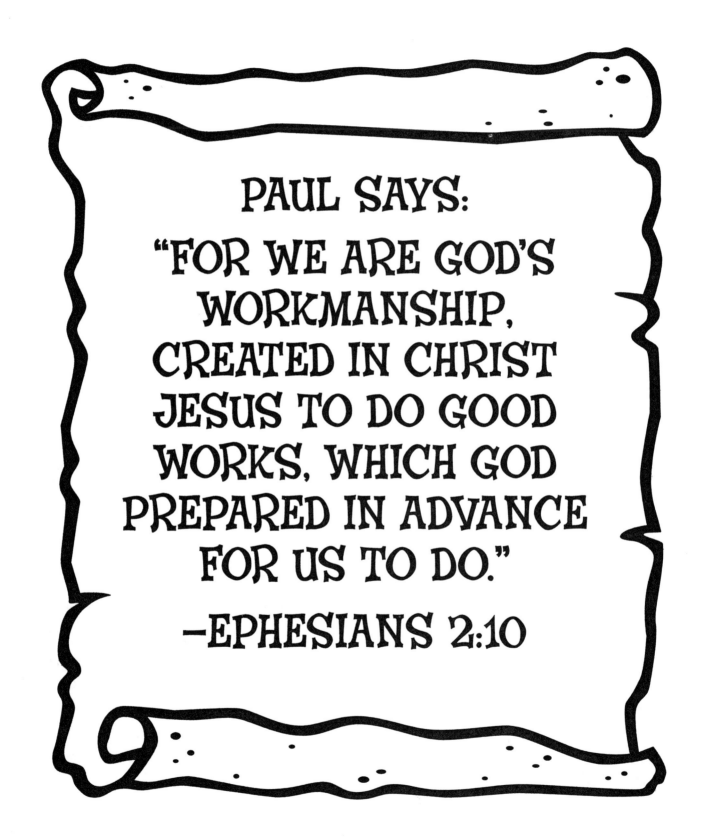

PAUL SAYS:

"FOR WE ARE GOD'S WORKMANSHIP, CREATED IN CHRIST JESUS TO DO GOOD WORKS, WHICH GOD PREPARED IN ADVANCE FOR US TO DO."

—EPHESIANS 2:10

SPECIAL DELIVERY MAIL

▼▼▼▼▼▼▼▼▼▼▼▼▼▼▼▼

▼
▼
▼
▼
▼
▼
▼
▼
▼
▼
▼
▼
▼
▼
▼
▼
▼
▼
▼
▼
▼
▼
▼

GIVE TO LIVE

LEADER'S DEVOTIONAL
▼▾▼▾▼▾▼▾▼▾▼▾▼

Dale is the youth pastor of the fastest growing junior high ministry in town. Every month at his ministry's concert outreach, scores of junior highers receive Christ. Then they get involved with amusement park trips, ski adventures, and river rafting weekends. Dale can hardly keep up with the number of converts in his group, so all he knows to do is add more and more social activities to keep students coming.

Robyn's junior high ministry isn't growing as quickly. Every month or two a junior higher will receive Christ and then get plugged into a small group. Every six months the group goes on a weeklong missions trip. Every year Robyn takes a handful of students on a weeklong discipleship and service retreat.

Fast forward ten years. Where are Dale's students? As twenty-three-year-olds, most have dropped away from church and are pursuing the highest paying careers and most attractive dating partners available.

What about Robyn's students? Most of them are involved in a local church ministry, wrestling with how to integrate their faith with their new jobs and trying to develop Christ-centered friendships.

What's the difference between Dale's and Robyn's students? The difference is that Dale's were converts, Robyn's were disciples.

A convert is someone who is going to heaven but isn't taking anyone with him. A disciple is someone who has been transformed by the

SESSION 5

grace of God and works to spread that grace to others. As we will examine in this session, in Jesus' last words, He didn't command His disciples to "make converts." He commanded them to "make disciples." Because they made disciples, the church spread and grew. Because they made disciples, who in turn made disciples, who in turn made disciples, you are teaching this lesson today. Your legacy is the group of students who point to you and say, "That person made me a disciple who disciples others."

KEY VERSES

"Then Jesus came to them and said, 'All authority in heaven and on earth has been given to me. Therefore go and make disciples of all nations, baptizing them in the name of the Father and of the Son and of the Holy Spirit, and teaching them to obey everything I have commanded you. And surely I am with you always, to the very end of the age.'" Matthew 28:18-20

BIBLICAL BASIS

Matthew 28:16-20; Acts 8:26-40

FOCUS OF THIS SESSION

God's gift to us is salvation and He asks us to share this good news with others.

AIMS OF THIS SESSION

During this session students will:
- Examine Christ's last commands to His disciples and their relevance to our gifts;
- Discover the importance of sharing the gift of God's salvation with others;
- Identify one unsaved friend to pray for this week.

APPROACH THE WORD

▼▼▼▼▼▼▼▼▼▼▼▼

(15 MINUTES)

OBJECTIVE

To help students understand the importance of following commands.

MATERIALS AND PREPARATION NEEDED

- ❑ Two unopened loaves of bread
- ❑ Jar of peanut butter
- ❑ Jar of jelly
- ❑ Knife
- ❑ Table
- ❑ Paper towels for cleanup

Before the session begins, set up the table with the food on it.

FOLLOWING DIRECTIONS

Be sure to warmly welcome your students to this last session and then ask: **How many of you like peanut-butter-and-jelly sandwiches? How many of you know how to make peanut-butter-and-jelly sandwiches?** Choose one male and one female volunteer who know how to make peanut-butter-and-jelly sandwiches to come to the front of the room.

Explain that instead of making the sandwich themselves, they are going to instruct you in how to make a sandwich. Send the female out of the room, then have the male student stand several feet in front of the table with his back to the table while you stand behind the table.

Ask the male to give you instructions on how to make a peanut-but-ter-and-jelly sandwich. The key is to follow his instructions exactly. For instance, if he doesn't say to remove the bread from the bag, everything he subsequently tells you to do to the bread must be done while the bread is still in the bag. Or if he says to spread the peanut butter on the bread, but doesn't say to use a knife to do so, you should use your fingers. Let the audience see what you are doing and how his instructions (which will inevitably be flawed and incomplete) lead to a pretty ridiculous sandwich.

SESSION 5

Once the male student has finished giving instructions, hold up your finished product for him to see. Then hide that sandwich and ask the female volunteer to come in and repeat the process.

Once she has finished, compare the two sandwiches with the class. Interview the two students and ask them:

How did it feel to have to give such precise instructions?

Were you worried that you might be wrong?

Then ask the class:

Why are instructions important?

Have you ever received some bad instructions or directions? What happened?

Transition to the rest of the lesson by explaining: **Today we're going to look at some directions that are absolutely foolproof. If you follow them, you will never go wrong.**

BIBLE EXPLORATION

▼▾▼▾▼▾▼▾▼▾▼▾▼▾

(35 MINUTES)

OBJECTIVE

To help students understand the importance of salvation and disciple making.

MATERIALS AND PREPARATION NEEDED

- ❏ Photocopy "Write Away" on page 86, one for every two students
- ❏ Pens or pencils
- ❏ Two small bags of M&M candies

Ahead of time, ask one of your junior highers or another church member to share a testimony of how he or she either had a chance to share the gift of salvation with someone else who became a Christian or how someone else shared the gift of salvation with them.

In addition, you may want to add a second testimony of someone who shared the gift of salvation with someone else, but that person didn't receive Christ.

Before class begins, give one small bag of M&Ms to one student and ask him or her not to open them until later.

WRITE AWAY

Explain: **Today we're going to look at the best instruction giver ever, Jesus Christ. His instructions never let you down. In fact, we're going to look at the very last things He said to His disciples after He was raised from the dead.**

Ask students to get into pairs and then distribute a pen or pencil and a copy of "Write Away" to each pair. Ask the pairs to *circle* any people mentioned in the passage, to *underline* any of Jesus' commands, and to *draw* a squiggly line under any of Jesus' promises. After giving them a minute or two to do so, ask one pair to share what words they underlined as Jesus' commands. Have another pair share Jesus' promises and a different pair share the people they circled.

Explain: **Jesus gives several commands in this passage, but the one that is most important is in verse 19: "Make disciples." What does it mean to make disciples? It means sharing the gift of your faith with someone, but it doesn't stop there. It also means helping them grow and mature in Christ. Then they in turn share their faith with others, and so on. Up until now, we've been talking about the spiritual gifts and abilities that are unique to each one of us. Now we're talking about a gift that any of us can share with others.**

Open up the small bag of M&Ms and explain: **It's as if each M&M represents sharing your faith.** Begin to pass out one M&M to each student and explain: **With each of you I am sharing my faith.** When you get to the student who has the small bag of M&Ms, have him or her stand up and explain: **Making disciples means that the people I share my faith with who accept Christ as Savior then share that gift with others.** Have him/her open the bag of M&Ms and share them with others.

Then ask the person(s) giving the testimony (or testimonies) to come forward and share for two to three minutes each about their experience in either sharing or receiving the gift of salvation.

Note: If you are completing this session in one meeting, ignore this break and skip to "Conclusion and Decision."

Session 5

Two-Meeting Track: If you want to spread this session over two meetings, STOP here and close in prayer. Inform students of the content to be covered in your next meeting.

Review and Approach

(15 Minutes)

Goal

To help students understand the importance of giving clear explanations.

Materials and Preparation Needed

❑ Photocopy one copy of "You Don't Say" on page 87
❑ Stopwatch or a watch that indicates seconds

Ahead of time, cut the "You Don't Say" page so that you have 16 separate "You Don't Say" cards.

You Don't Say

To begin this session, ask for two male and two female volunteers. Explain that they are going to play "You Don't Say" (this game is similar to the popular game "Taboo"). You will give each volunteer a stack of four cards, which they are not to look at in advance. You are going to time the volunteers to see how long it takes them to get their team to guess the word on each card that is above the line through a verbal description. The words that are below the line are the ones You Don't Say and the volunteer cannot use them in his or her verbal description. If they use one of these words, add 10 seconds to their time. Absolutely no hand motions are allowed.

Once you explain the rules, have the first male volunteer describe his four cards one at a time to the male students. The female students must remain silent. Keep track of how long it takes him to get his team to guess all four cards. Repeat the process for the female students.

Repeat for the second round with the last two volunteers. Total the time for males and for females and declare a winner.

Discuss:

Why was this game so tough?

When is it also hard to describe something?

Transition to the rest of the lesson by explaining: **We want to make sure that you know how to describe the most important gift ever, the gift of salvation through Christ. By the time you leave today, you will be able to explain that gift to anyone.**

BIBLE EXPLORATION TWO

(30 MINUTES)

OBJECTIVE

To give students a tool and the skills to share their faith as Philip did.

MATERIALS AND PREPARATION NEEDED

- ❑ Two metal trash cans
- ❑ Some firewood
- ❑ Paper
- ❑ Matches
- ❑ One 10-inch piece of heavy string per student
- ❑ Yellow beads
- ❑ Black beads
- ❑ Red beads
- ❑ White beads
- ❑ Green beads

Ahead of time, put some firewood in each metal trash can.

ON FIRE

Ask for a volunteer to read Acts 8:26-40. Ask the class: **What role did Philip have in the Ethiopian receiving the gift of salvation through Christ?** Get their answers and explain: **God didn't need Philip to reach** the Ethiopian. In fact, He doesn't need us to reach anyone. He could spread the Good News by dropping flyers from the sky or through an internet chat room. And yet He chooses to use us to share the gift of salvation with others.

Indicate both trash cans with the firewood inside. Light a match or two and drop them into one of the trash cans and explain: **This wood will catch on fire just as it is.** Then hold up some paper and say: **And yet the paper will probably help the wood catch on fire a little faster and a little easier. Since Philip was willing to explain the story about Jesus to the Ethiopian, he acted like this paper to help facilitate the fire.** Drop the paper into the second trash can, light it on fire, and see how much quicker the second trash can ignites. You may want to practice this ahead of time to make sure your technique produces the desired results. You may also want to check for smoke alarms that might go off (or do this outside).

Like Philip, how many of you could explain the story of Jesus right now? Ask for volunteers to do so. Explain: **By the end of this lesson, you will be like Philip because you will be able to explain the gift of salvation through Jesus.** Then give a piece of string and one bead of each color to your students. Have them tie a knot about two inches from the end of their string. Then ask them to put a yellow bead on the thread so that it sits just above the knot as you explain: **The yellow bead represents the power and love of God.** Have them put the black bead on next as you explain: **The black bead represents our sin that separates us from God.** Then the red bead as you continue: **This represents the blood of Jesus that was shed for us two thousand years ago.** Then the white bead: **If we confess our sins and believe that He is the risen Savior, and ask Him to take over our lives, then He cleanses our sin and makes us as clean as this bead.** And finally, as they place the green bead on last, explain: **The last bead is green because once we are in Christ, we are new creatures and we can grow just like a plant.** Ask them to tie a knot above the green bead, and then give them a minute to help one another tie the bracelets on their wrists.

CONCLUSION AND DECISION

▼▼▼▼▼▼▼▼▼▼▼▼▼

(15 MINUTES)

OBJECTIVE

To give students who have not received the gift of Christ a chance to do so. To ask all students to commit to sharing the gift of Christ with a friend.

MATERIALS AND PREPARATION NEEDED

- ❑ One large package wrapped in white paper
- ❑ Felt-tip pen

Explain: **Some of you have not made a decision yourself to receive the gift of salvation through Christ. If you'd like to do that now, I'd like to lead you in this prayer aloud, asking you to repeat after me. If you've already prayed to receive the gift of salvation through Christ, please recite the prayer aloud as a sign of your ongoing commitment to Him.**

Read the prayer, making sure you stop every few words so students can repeat:

Dear Jesus, I know that I have sinned, and I need Your forgiveness. I ask You to come into my life and take control. By Your grace please help me to follow You as Your disciple. And Lord, as I grow in You, help me make disciples of others. Amen.

Hold up the wrapped package and explain: **This package represents the gift of salvation that we can share with others. Do you know anyone who needs to hear about this gift? If so, I'm going to pass the gift and a pen around the room and I'd like you to write that person's name on the gift as a commitment to pray for that person this week and to look for an opportunity to share about the gift of Christ.** Lead the way by writing someone's name yourself.

You may want to lead in worship music while the gift and pen are circulating. Close in prayer, asking God to use the students to share the gift of salvation with others.

WRITE AWAY
▼▾▼▾▼▾▼▾▼▾▼▾▼▾▼

Work with your partner to do the following:

❑ Circle all the people mentioned in this passage.
❑ Underline any of Jesus' commands.
❑ Draw a squiggly line under any of Jesus' promises.

Then the eleven disciples went to Galilee, to the mountain where Jesus had told them to go. When they saw him, they worshiped him; but some doubted. Then Jesus came to them and said, "All authority in heaven and on earth has been given to me. Therefore go and make disciples of all nations, baptizing them in the name of the Father and of the Son and of the Holy Spirit, and teaching them to obey everything I have commanded you. And surely I am with you always, to the very end of the age." —Matthew 28:16-20

You Don't Say

▼▼▼▼▼▼▼▼▼▼▼▼▼▼

Shoe	**Pizza**	**Pen**	**Watch**
You Don't Say	*You Don't Say*	*You Don't Say*	*You Don't Say*
Foot	Cheese	Ink	Wrist
Leather	Italian	Paper	Time
Tennis	Crust	Write	Wear
Trash	**Lunch**	**Nail Polish**	**Jeans**
You Don't Say	*You Don't Say*	*You Don't Say*	*You Don't Say*
Can	Noon	Finger	Pants
Garbage	Breakfast	Paint	Denim
Truck	Dinner	Color	Wear
Book	**Swimming Pool**	**Egg**	**Fourth of July**
You Don't Say	*You Don't Say*	*You Don't Say*	*You Don't Say*
Paper	Summer	Chicken	Fireworks
Read	Hot	Yolk	America
School	Bathing suit	Scrambled	Independence
February	**Elephant**	**Road**	**Seatbelt**
You Don't Say	*You Don't Say*	*You Don't Say*	*You Don't Say*
Month	Trunk	Cars	Car
Valentine's Day	Grey	Street	Waist
March	Tusks	Drive	Safe